IRISH WIT

quips and quotes

TOM HAY

summersdale

IRISH WIT

Summersdale Publishers Ltd
46 West Street
Chichester
West Sussex
PO19 1RP
UK

www.summersdale.com

Printed and bound in Singapore

ISBN: 978-1-84024-731-2

Contents

Editor's Note   5

Insults   7

Ireland and the Irish   15

Eating and Drinking   24

Love and Marriage   33

Work and Money   42

The English and Other Foreigners   48

Sport   54

Religion   60

Life   67

The Big Sleep   74

Politics   82

The Arts   90

Editor's Note

Sean O'Casey once said of his countrymen that 'they treat a joke as a serious thing, and a serious thing as a joke'. Hardly surprising, then, that Irish wit and logic is renowned the world over.

From George Bernard Shaw to Brendan Behan, the Emerald Isle boasts an abundance of wit-smiths: within these pages alone you'll find more laughs than you can shake a shamrock at.

Oscar Wilde once quite rightly pointed out that, 'Life is much too important a thing ever to talk seriously about it'; as the mirthful musings in this book show, the same rule applies to eating and drinking, love and marriage, work and money, and so much more…

Insults

In the human race, you came last.

Spike Milligan

I loved her so much I named my first ulcer after her.

Dusty Young

If you had a brain cell it would die of loneliness.

John O'Dwyer

*She has an ego like
a raging tooth.*

W. B. Yeats

*He'd be out of his depth
on a wet pavement.*

Joe O'Shea

No, that skirt doesn't make you look fatter. How could it?

Maureen Potter

Simon Cowell's waxwork in Madame Tussauds is more real than he is.

Louis Walsh

Your features don't seem to know the value of teamwork.

Gene Fitzpatrick

The only thing my husband ever achieved on his own was his moustache.

Jane O'Reilly

Why don't you write books people can read?

Nora Joyce to her husband James

If I say that he's extremely stupid, I don't mean that in any derogatory sense.

Brendan O'Carroll

For a young girl to be named 'wholesome' is perhaps the deadliest insult of all.

Caitlin Thomas

Ireland and
the Irish

*An Irishman was once
asked to define winter.
'It's the time of year,'
he explained, 'when
it gets late early.'*

Tom McIntyre

Irish women like the simple things in life – like Irish men.

Mary Coughlan

Never hit an Irishman when he's down. He might get up again.

Seamus O'Leary

*Dublin University contains
the cream of Ireland
– rich and thick.*

Samuel Beckett

*The Irish, and I'm also
guilty of this, think they
invented everything.*

Bono

Being Irish, he had an abiding sense of tragedy, which sustained him through temporary periods of joy.

William Butler Yeats

A secret in Dublin means just telling one person at a time.

Ciarán MacGonigal

I'm Irish. We think sideways.

Spike Milligan

The Irish love to be loved,
except by each other.

David Kenny

The inner city architecture
of Dublin is like a lady in the
morning without her make-up on.

Jim Tunney

When anyone asks me about the Irish character, I say look at the trees. Maimed, stark and misshapen, but ferociously tenacious.

Edna O'Brien

It's not that the Irish are cynical. It's simply that they have a wonderful lack of respect for everything and everybody.

Brendan Behan

That's the Irish people all over – they treat a joke as a serious thing, and a serious thing as a joke.

Sean O'Casey

An Irishman was asked if the Irish always answered one question with another. 'Who told you that?' he replied.

Niall Toibin

Eating and Drinking

How do you cross Dublin

without passing a pub?

Go into all of them!

James Joyce, *Ulysses*

Never eat on an empty stomach.

Jason Byrne

Drink is your enemy.
Love your enemies.

Sil Fox

*It was a bold man who
ate the first oyster.*

Jonathan Swift

*A hot dog feeds the
hand that bites it.*

Derek Davis

*The only reason I went
to America was because
I saw a sign saying
'Drink Canada Dry'.*

George Best

I lost so many years through drink, it was 1972 before I learned JFK had been assassinated.

David Kelly

A restaurant I used to frequent in Cork advertised: 'Eat here and you'll never eat anywhere else again.'

Niall Toibin

In England I'm regarded as an alcoholic. In Ireland they see me as a sissy drinker.

Shane MacGowan

I finally found a diet that works in Ireland. I only eat when the weather's good.

Hal Roach

Only in Ireland is the pint of stout regarded as a digestif.

Terry Wogan

In 1969 I gave up drinking and sex. It was the worst 20 minutes of my life.

George Best

*I didn't fight my way to
the top of the food chain
to be a vegetarian.*

Joe O'Herlihy

*Abstinence should always be
practised in moderation.*

Joe Lynch

Love and
Marriage

A man who says his wife can't take a joke forgets that she took him.

Oscar Wilde

*Foreplay, in Ireland, is
the technical term for
taking your shoes off.*

Joseph O'Connor

*I wonder what fool it was
that first invented kissing?*

Jonathan Swift

Love may make the world go round, but not as fast as whisky.

Richard Harris

*Marriage is forever
– like cement.*

Peter O'Toole

*Safe sex to a Dubliner is doing it
when your wife's gone to bingo.*

David Kenny

*We had a quiet wedding.
Her father had a silencer
on the shotgun.*

Sean Kilroy

Give women the vote and in five years' time there will be a crushing tax on bachelors.

George Bernard Shaw

I think, therefore I'm single.

Sinead Flynn

If there were no husbands, who would look after our mistresses?

George Moore

*I'm hoarse listening to
my wife complaining.*

Brendan Behan

*Never make a task a pleasure,
as the man said when he dug his
wife's grave only three feet deep.*

Seamus McManus

I don't tell my wife anything.
I figure that what she doesn't
know won't hurt me.

Danny Cummins

I'm giving up marriage for Lent.

Brian Behan

Work and
Money

The only really dirty four-lettered word is 'work'.

Brendan Kennelly

My father is so long on the dole he thinks a P45 is a gun.

Big O

I have never liked working. To me a job is an invasion of privacy.

Danny McGoorty

The only thing that has to be finished by next Friday is next Thursday.

Maureen Potter

Money couldn't buy friends, but you get a better class of enemy.

Spike Milligan

*A man's respect for law
and order exists in precise
relationship to the size
of his pay cheque.*

Adam Clayton

*If anyone broke into our house,
they'd leave a donation.*

Frank Carson

*Nothing is more expensive
than a girl who's free
for the evening.*

Hal Roach

The English
and Other
Foreigners

The English character is fearful of intellectuals in a way that Dracula had a thing about crosses.

Declan Lynch

The British beatitudes are beer, business, bibles, bulldogs, battleships, buggery and bishops.

James Joyce

The Irish remember too much and the English too little.

Eilis O'Hanlon

For many years I thought an innuendo was an Italian suppository.

Spike Milligan

Americans will go on adoring me until I say something nice about them.

George Bernard Shaw

We have really everything in common with America nowadays except, of course, language.

Oscar Wilde, *The Canterville Ghost*

De Valera is the greatest Irishman born in New York to a Spanish father who ever lived.

Pat Fitzpatrick

A Mexican straight flush is any five cards and a gun.

Hugh Leonard

Sport

Old golfers don't die.

They just putter out.

Sil Fox

Chelsea has just launched a new aftershave called 'The Special One' by U Go Boss.

Pat Flanagan on José Mourinho's departure
from the football club in 2007

A golf club is a stick with a head on one end and a fool on the other.

Damien Muldoon

*My idea of exercise is striking
a match for a cigarette.*

Anne-Marie Scanlon

*It's always nice to start
off with a good result.*

Robbie Keane

I gave up shadow-boxing the night my shadow beat me up.

James McKeon

Peter Clohessy's main problem was that he couldn't stop jumping on hookers.

Dermot Morgan

Show me a dressing room of nice polite players and I'll show you a dressing room full of losers.

Tony Cascarino

Religion

Opportunity only knocks once. If there's a second one, it's probably a Jehovah's Witness.

John O'Connor

*Irish atheists have started a
'Dial-A-Prayer' service. When
they phone, nobody answers.*

Hal Roach

*I'm terrified about the day that
I enter the gates of heaven and
God says to me: just a minute.*

Maureen O'Hara

Ireland remains a deeply divided country, the two main denominations being 'us' and 'them'.

Frank McNally

When did I realise I was God? Well, I was praying and I suddenly realised I was talking to myself.

Peter O'Toole

I'm an Irish Catholic and I have a long iceberg of guilt.

Edna O'Brien

When the gods want to punish us, they answer our prayers.

Oscar Wilde

I'm an Atheist...
thank God.

Dave Allen

Every saint has a past and every sinner a future.

Callum Best

How I wish that Adam had died with all his bones in his body!

Dion Boucicault

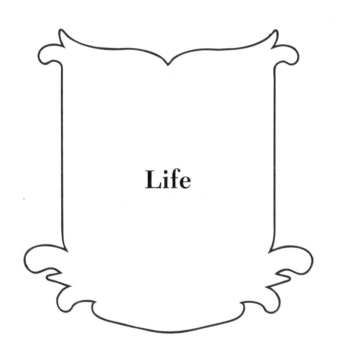

Life

I'm not so sure if I believe in reincarnation. I can't even remember the things I've done in this life.

Richard Harris

Every dog has its day, but only a dog with a broken tail has a weak end.

Seamus O'Leary

Life is a long preparation for something that never happens.

William Butler Yeats

What do I know of man's destiny? I could tell you more about radishes.

Samuel Beckett

Life is much too important a thing ever to talk seriously about it.

Oscar Wilde

I would like to divide my life into alternating periods of penance, cavorting and work.

Edna O'Brien

We're not the men our fathers were. If we were we would be terribly old.

Flann O'Brien

Every man desires to live long,
but no man wishes to be old.

Jonathan Swift

Glory is fleeting, but
obscurity is forever.

Thomas Moore

All I want to do is sit on my arse, fart and think of Dante.

Samuel Beckett

The day after tomorrow is the third day of the rest of your life.

George Carlin

The Big
Sleep

I intend to die in bed at 110 writing poetry, sipping Guinness and serenading a woman.

Richard Harris

*I'm not afraid of dying
– I just don't want to be
there when it happens.*

Spike Milligan

*If my father was alive to
see the modern world,
he'd turn in his grave.*

Michael O'Doherty

I watched a funeral go by and asked who was dead. A man said, 'The fella in the box.'

Dave Allen

I am told he makes a very handsome corpse, and becomes his coffin prodigiously.

Oliver Goldsmith

An undertaker is the last man to let you down.

Jimmy O'Dea

There's no point taking out life insurance. My uncle did and he died all the same.

Sean Kilroy

A doctor's reputation is made by the number of eminent men who die under his care.

George Bernard Shaw

*My grandmother made
dying her life's work.*

Hugh Leonard

*Either that wallpaper
goes, or I do.*

Oscar Wilde's last words

I told you I was ill.

Spike Milligan's epitaph

Funerals in Ireland are so jolly,
they should be called funferalls.

James Joyce

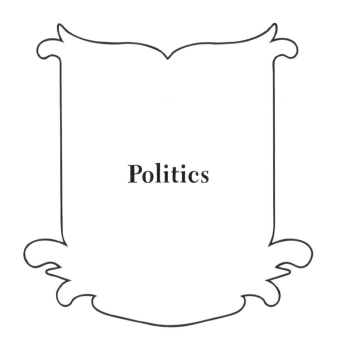

Politics

The weak are a long time in politics.

Barry Egan

If the word 'No' was removed from the English language, Ian Paisley would be speechless.

John Hume

He knows nothing and thinks he knows everything. That clearly points to a career in politics.

George Bernard Shaw

Don't vote. The government always gets in.

Frank Kelly

Making peace, I have found, is much harder than making war.

Gerry Adams

Arnold Schwarzenegger is the governor of California. He got there by lifting things.

Dylan Moran

Ireland has the best politicians money can buy.

Sam Snort

My electioneering style? I kiss the mothers and shake hands with the babies.

Joe Costello

*A man should always be
drunk when he talks of
politics. It's the only way
to make them important.*

Seán O'Casey

*Why do you stand for
election to get a seat?*

Donal Foley

The Greeks came up with democracy, but they had no intention of everyone having it.

Bono

If Irish politicians were laid end to end, they'd have their feet in each other's mouths.

Seamus O'Leary

The Arts

Sleep is an excellent way of listening to an opera.

James Stephens

Writing is like getting married.
One should never commit oneself
until one is amazed at one's luck.

Iris Murdoch

Never judge a book by its movie.

Cyril Cusack

Memoirs are a well-known form of fiction.

Frank Harris

If there's music in hell, it'll be bagpipes.

Joe Tomelty

A poet can survive anything but a misprint.

Oscar Wilde

Murder is considered less immoral than fornication in literature.

George Moore

I write like a snail trailing slime. But sometimes the slime glistens.

John Banville

www.summersdale.com